MOTHER NATURE
GOES NUTS!

Amazing Natural Disasters

KLUTZ.

What's This Book About?

This is a book about Mother Nature on her really *really* bad days, when she's feeling absolutely rotten. The book is broken into six sections, each of them on the subject of one kind of natural disaster or another: tornadoes, hurricanes, earthquakes, tsunamis, floods, and volcanoes. Each section contains stories told by survivors, the most amazing photos we could find, and a dose of "disasterology," the science behind it all.

Tornadoes

Tornadoes are at the far end of what's possible in extreme weather. Highly unpredictable and incredibly powerful, tornadoes are barely believable. The windspeed of a tornado's interior has never been properly measured, but radar-based estimates run around 318 mph — enough to drive a yardstick into a tree like a nail and to cause woodframe buildings to basically explode.

Hurricanes

Compared to quick-jab tornadoes, hurricanes are slow-footed sluggers — big and powerful, but you can see them coming. In North America, they're usually born between June and November in the mid-Atlantic Ocean. Katrina, probably the most disastrous North American hurricane of the past 100 years, has come to symbolize a number of things, but "modern weather going crazy" is primary among them.

Earthquakes

The molten core of the planet is covered by an earth-crust that slides and skids around a little bit more than those of us who ride on it would prefer. Fasten your seatbelts.

Up until December 26, 2004, tsunamis were considered dangerous but extremely rare. Today, they're considered a lot more dangerous and a little less rare. The tsunami created that day by an earthquake centered in the Indian Ocean was one of the most destructive and deadly natural disasters of modern times.

We live on a thin skin of rock and earth floating on a planet whose center is unimaginably hot. Every once in a while, we get a violent reminder of that when a crack forms and we get an enormous volcanic squirt of what lies beneath.

Water + dirt make mud. Nearly every year, around the world, a massive dose of that recipe accounts for more damage than all other natural disasters. Floods are Number One in the money loss (and mess created) categories.

Introduction

Taking the "Natural" Out of "Natural Disasters"

If you're a big fan of extreme and crazy weather, you've definitely picked the right time to be alive. The last ten years have been huge: the tsunami of Indonesia in 2004; the floods associated with hurricane Katrina in 2005; the on-going droughts in Africa and southeast U.S., and the incredible hurricane season of North America in 2005. All in all, these are the best of times for the worst of weather.

It's not entirely luck, of course. Human activity has been crucially involved, especially over the last two hundred years. We have a very large appetite for energy and we get most of it from the burning of coal and oil. That process releases carbon dioxide and other greenhouse gasses in a way that has caused the planet's overall temperature to begin rising in a frightening way.

But individual storms (like hurricane Katrina, to take the most famous example) do not really belong in the global warming discussion. This Tuesday's weather is way too specific to get into a conversation about a change as huge and complicated as global warming.

Here's an analogy: In these days of better nutrition and health care, humans are generally taller than they once were. But even so, that is not the key reason behind the fact that Joe Crabtree, of Ft. Bend, Indiana, is 6'6".

When you get away from individual events, however, and start looking at trends and averages, it's a very different story. The trend towards bigger, Category 5–type hurricanes is well documented and scientists are now quite suspicious that the culprit is warmer ocean water caused by global warming. Whether droughts and floods are connected to global warming in the same way is still under debate, although the parallels are suspicious. The underlying reality is that over the past 200 years we have burned trillions of tons of coal and oil. And on a planet like ours, where every system is connected to every other system, that has repercussions. We are just now starting to see what they are and what exactly it is that we've done. It's not nice to mess with Mother Nature.

Ever wonder what the biggest source of greenhouse gasses is?

And now for a word about the climate change debate...

There isn't one. Not about the basic questions. The fact that the earth's climate is warming and that trend is in large part a consequence of human industry is scientifically established. No serious group of informed climate scientists disagrees with that statement. None.

Of course, with over 6 billion people on the planet, it's hard to get a group of that size to agree 100% on anything. Consequently, there continue to be many (well-publicized) people who refuse to believe in the existence of climate change. (For an interesting read in this context, check out the Wikipedia entry on the Flat Earth Society, founded in the mid-1800's in England and most recently headquartered in Lancaster, CA. They believe the Earth is a flat disc bounded by a large wall of ice. It's an interesting point of view. But a minority one.)

The largest study on the questions of global climate change was done by the Intergovernmental Panel on Climate Change. It was completed and released in 2007, the same year the group received a share of the Nobel Peace Prize. Hundreds of climate scientists from around the globe contributed, making it one of the larger scientific studies ever performed on any issue. Obviously there are many details still under debate and a consensus view may never emerge on many of them. But on some key issues, there is very broad agreement. Here are some of those:

- **The earth's climate is changing and getting warmer.**

- **Human-produced carbon dioxide is the leading cause.**

- **Arctic ice is disappearing at a rate never before seen in modern times.**

- **Glaciers are retreating in the same unprecedented way.**

- **Sea levels will rise as a consequence.** How much is impossible to predict with complete accuracy today.

- **A failure to reverse, or at least slow, this trend will have very serious unforeseeable consequences** for the entire planet and its inhabitants. That would be you and me.

What's Your Carbon Footprint?

In this day and age, you really have to know only three things about yourself: Your email address, your cell phone number, and your carbon footprint.

What's your carbon footprint?

It's the amount of carbon you burn to get you through your day. If you spend your day flying in an overheated private jet, under an electric blanket, eating exotically grown foods, drinking French water, wearing typically manufactured clothes, and drying your hair and nails with an electric hair dryer… you've left a big footprint on the planet that day.

If you've spent your day shivering and starving in a cave, you've left a very small one.

If you've spent your day doing something in the middle, you've left another-sized footprint.

Making sure that mid-sized footprint is no bigger than it has to be, should be everybody's modern goal. It's just like picking up the trash when you leave the picnic. Only a lot more important. The rule: Every day, in every way, watch your footprint.

Average North American creates 5.6 tons of carbon each year.

Average Chinese citizen creates 1 ton of carbon each year.

Average African creates 0.34 tons of carbon each year.

Average European creates 2.13 tons of carbon each year.

Average South American creates 0.71 tons of carbon each year.

A Brain-Saver Quiz

Ten questions, but we'll spot you nine

In our never-ending quest to save energy, we've invented "Brain-Saver Quizzes." What's the difference between "Brain-Saver Quizzes" and regular, old-fashioned quizzes? Simple! Ours come with almost all the answers provided! How great is that!

Take this "Brain Saver Quiz" and see how you do. Good luck!

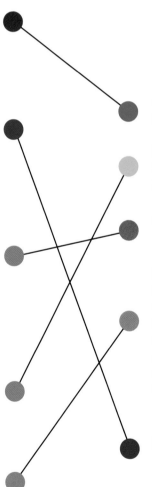

If the rate of population growth doesn't change, in about 2,400 years, the planet Earth will be…

The Australian government is intent on ridding the entire country of them. In fact, they will be officially banned by law starting in the year 2010. They are…

Daylight Savings Time provides an extra hour of sunlight for the Earth. Scientists invented it so that solar cells would work better and for longer.

"It's not that unusual," said European scientist Slavisa Ignjatovic. He was talking about something that rained down from the sky during a violent storm the previous day.

El Nino is:

a packed ball of human flesh expanding outward at the speed of light

(A) meatballs, (B) wet Bulgarian money, PICK ME **(C) frogs, (D) semi-precious stones**

T or (F)

(A) the finishing move of Mexico City wrestler El Monstro, (B) a South American dance fad, (C) the Aztec god of NASCAR racing, PICK ME **(D) a rise in surface water temperature in the central and eastern Pacific that has a profound effect on climate and weather throughout the world. Happens every 2–7 years.**

Circle one

By the end of this century, scientists believe that weather forecasters will…

Typhoons are…

A "cock-eyed bob" is…

Wind is caused primarily by…

In ancient times, floods were much less a problem than today because…

(A) be able to predict the weather in their sleep, (B) be extinct. Weather will be controlled by Congress, (C) be 99% percent accurate, PICK ME ☞ (D) not be a lot more accurate than they are today. Weather is fundamentally chaotic and impossible to predict with 100% accuracy. Period.

(A) the mere fact that the Earth spins, (B) the whims of ancient and often angry weather gods, (C) the wing flappings of millions of migrating birds, PICK ME ☞ (D) the constant changing of air pressure usually driven by changes in land temperature

(A) a plastic surgery procedure intended to move your eyes and chin a little closer, (B) the state cocktail of Nebraska, (C) an arctic seabird with a "sarcastic, anti-social attitude," PICK ME ☞ (D) the Australian word for "tornado"

(A) rich business guys, (B) a small Indonesian jungle animal that survives entirely on 7-Up and bamboo, (C) the Taiwanese word for "village idiot," PICK ME ☞ (D) the word used for hurricanes when they happen in Asia

(A) it didn't rain very much in ancient times, (B) the word for "flood" hadn't been invented yet, (C) before the invention of swimming pools, people liked floods, PICK ME ☞ (D) ancient people made no effort to control river flows so they avoided building in places that tended to flood

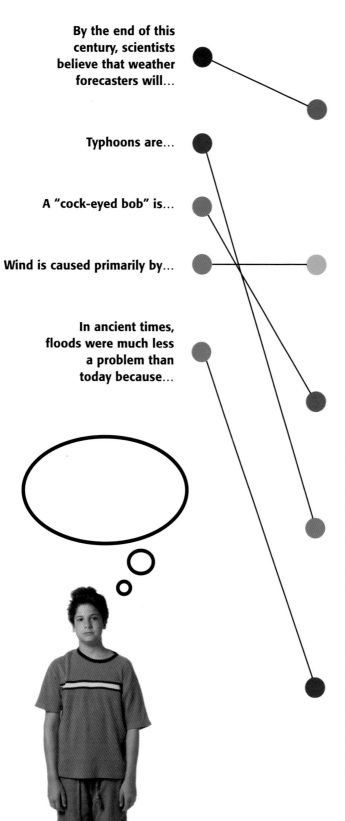

WORLD'S POPULATION

2000 — 6.2 Billion

The Only Graph in This Book

The idea that humans can influence climate is an extremely modern idea; newer than computers actually. For the last 100,000 years it would have been a joke. How many humans does it take to make the moon come up? How many humans does it take to make the weather different?

Unfortunately, we've learned the answer and now it's not very funny: somewhere between 6 and 7 billion.

But it's actually not true. The planet can support a population of that size and larger if other numbers don't tag along. Here are the important figures: 40,000 million barrels of oil and 4,000 million tons of coal. That's how much fossil fuel we currently consume every year. But the encouraging fact is this: The world's population can grow at the same time those numbers come down. Global climate change is not an inevitable consequence of population growth.

It's not the size of the population, it's the kind.

Year 1000 — 500 Million

Year 1500 — 500 Million

Year 500 — 400 Million

Year Zero — 300 Million

500 B.C.

Portrait of a Monster

Not all tornadoes are created equal.

Take this one pictured here, a tornado that hit Hesston, Kansas, in 1990. On the Fujita scale (see sidebar), it's an F-5, making it both an official monster and an extremely rare beast. Ninety percent of all tornadoes are in the F-1 – F-3 category. It's only when conditions are perfect that an F-5 develops. But when it happens, the result is like a combination freight train and bomb, a perfect storm.

A few of the more notorious F-5s are:

- The Flint, Michigan, tornado of June 8, 1953. The storm system that produced it moved on and spawned another tornado that hit Worcester, Massachusetts, the next day, for a true double whammy.

- The Waco, Texas, tornado of May 11, 1953. It demolished, among other things, a six-story furniture store and put to rest the old Native American belief that a tornado would never hit Waco.

- The Super Outbreak of April 3, 1974, in which 148 tornadoes hit 13 states. Six of those tornadoes were F-5 monsters.

RATE THE TORNADO

Scientists use the Fujita scale to rate tornadoes from F-1 to F-5, based on the damage they do.

F-1: Winds 73–112 mph (117–180 km/h)
Chimneys, tree branches and signs
are at risk.

F-2: Winds 113–157 mph (181–253 km/h)
Pushes moving cars off roads and mobile
homes off foundations. May destroy garages.

F-3: Winds 158–206 mph (254–332 km/h)
Tears roofs off houses, snaps or
uproots trees, demolishes mobile homes.

F-4: Winds 207–260 mph (333–419 km/h)
Tears roofs and walls off houses,
overturns trains and uproots many trees.

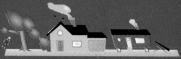

F-5: Winds 261 mph (420 km/h) and over
Lifts houses off foundations and carries them, makes cars
fly through the air, strips the bark off trees.

The Fujita scale is named
after its creator, the late
Dr. T. Theodore Fujita.
Here, he is pictured
watching a mini-tornado
made in his lab.

Flying Roofs and Air-Plucked Chickens

A roofless house is a fairly common sight in the track of a tornado. The reason? A combination of carpentry and aerodynamics.

Peaked roofs behave like poorly designed aircraft wings. The wind flows over them, reducing the pressure on top, giving the roof an upward lift. If the wind is strong enough, the nails will pull up and away goes the roof.

An Experiment

Huff and Puff and...

...prove that moving air can lift things. Hold a piece of paper by one end right in front of your mouth. Blow over the top and the drooping end will lift up.

Chickens that survive tornadoes are often found in a semi-plucked condition. The phenomenon is so common that one experimenter (in 1842) suggested that the strength of a tornado be rated depending on the number of feathers it manages to strip from its chicken victims. He even went so far as to launch a dead (but still feathered) chicken out of a cannon. Unfortunately, the chicken ended up in small, hard-to-find pieces, making conclusions about its feathers a little hard to figure. Modern scientists have since dropped the theory because chickens, when frightened, shed feathers all on their own, even without a tornado.

Pre-tornado

Survivor

(barely)

Post-tornado

Why Is This Man Smiling?

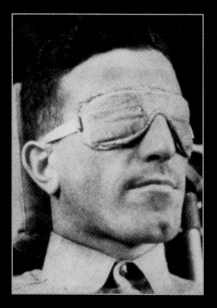
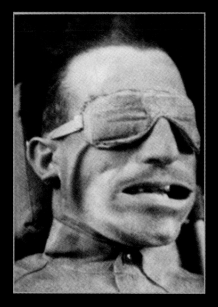
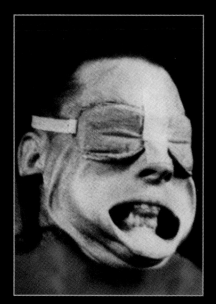

The Navy once ran a series of experiments to find out what happens when pilots eject from their aircraft at flight speeds. In the first round, a mannequin with a leather mask was placed before a special wind machine and the dial turned up to 300 mph (about 480 km/h). (Coincidentally, this is about the top measured speed in a tornado.) The mask ripped to shreds. In the second round, a volunteer stood in for the mannequin. His face, you'll be relieved to know, stayed on and even returned to normal.

Tess Bentley had only a few seconds before her home in Haines City, Florida, was hit by a tornado. She used those precious seconds to dive into her closet ("The closet actually came to me more than I came to it"). The storm ripped her mobile home off its foundation, gave it a ride, turned it upside-down and dumped it onto her neighbor's. Injuries? Nothing too serious. Even her porcelain angel collection survived ("I truly believe I have an angel watching over me").

We know of only one person who can answer the question: "What does the interior of a tornado look like?" Kansas farmer Will Keller reached the door of his storm cellar only a few seconds before the twister reached him. In the instant before he closed the door, he had a glimpse of something very few have ever lived to tell about: the insides of a tornado. He reported a screaming, hollow tube made of black swirling clouds, with lightning that zigzagged from side to side.

Amazing Survival Stories

The Homemade
Tornado Machine

By carefully following these directions, you can build a machine that will launch tiny twisters at people across the room. And irritate them.

1 Start with a cardboard tube. The best kind are oatmeal containers. Get rid of the oatmeal somehow. Then, cut a small circular hole in the bottom. Put it dead center, and make it about 1 inch (2.5 cm) across.

2 Cover the other end of the container (the open end) with a sheet of thin rubber. (We used an old balloon.) Secure it tightly in place with a rubber band — it should be as tight as a drum.

3 You're all set. Point your tube at some unsuspecting soul across the room. Snap the rubber bottom by pulling back on it and releasing. A tiny twister will come out of the other end and, if your aim is any good, hit your victim with a little puff.

rubber band

balloon

oatmeal box

cut a 1-inch hole

SAFETY NOTE: Adult supervision is required for this activity. Have an adult help cut the hole in the cardboard. Balloons are a choking hazard, and children under 8 can suffocate on uninflated balloons.

doughnut of compressed air

HOW COME IT WORKS?

When you snap the rubber on the bottom of the tube, you launch a bullet of compressed air out the hole on the other side. The confusing bit? The bullet gets turned inside out when it collides with the still air of the room.

An analogy? The doughnut hole becomes the doughnut. The doughnut stays intact as it travels because it's made of spinning air. Technically speaking, the doughnut is a tornado grabbing its own tail.

At 1:30 in the afternoon on Friday, August 16, 1993, a tornado touched down beside the front door of the Wal-Mart in Colonial Heights, Virginia, and proceeded to carve a neat slice of near-total destruction through the diapers, lingerie and Kathy Lee Gifford Collection. Moments later, the storm lifted off near the back exit. One employee said it felt like two seconds, but was probably about fifteen. To see what the store looked like afterward, turn the page.

WAL-MART

TORNADO *Trivia*

Storm Chasers

They call them "storm chasers," and when tornado season starts, they keep their trucks ready and their radios tuned to the weather station.

At the first tornado warning, they're off and running — *toward* the sighting. It's a high-thrill sport. If you're interested, you can sign up with an outfitter whose promise reads: "Travel with us, where the weather *really* sucks."

Tornado Alley

About one-third of the world's tornadoes occur in this part of the USA.

Dust Devils

On a really hot day, the sun beats down on the ground and heats it like a frying pan. The air directly above this hot spot also heats up and will sometimes spiral up toward the cooler air (obeying the hot-air-rises rule). If the ground is loose sand, the spiraling wind picks it up, making a dust devil.

Big dust devils hundreds of feet tall are fairly rare but mini-devils are around all the time, often powered by no more than the wind turning the corner of a building.

A Hail of a Storm

The violent thunderstorms that produce tornadoes sometimes also spit out hail. Hail forms when bits of dust or pollution get whisked up and down in the strong updrafts of a thunderstorm and are coated with layer upon layer of ice.

Some hailstones are whoppers. On June 22, 2003, the town of Aurora, Nebraska, was thumped with hailstones the size of volleyballs. Even bigger ones, about the size of pumpkins, fell in Bangladesh in 1986.

Waterspouts

▲ A tornado-like swirling column of water is called a waterspout. Sometimes these form when land tornadoes pass across water and suck up a drink. But most often, waterspouts start when swirling winds from above stir up a patch of the water's surface. If the winds continue, they can build into a fully formed spout. Waterspouts have been known to pick up fish and even small boats, lift them out of the water and give them a spin.

Oklahoma City, Tornado Town USA

It's an honor most cities would rather not have — City Most Likely To Be Hit By a Tornado. And the winner is… Oklahoma City, Oklahoma. Since 1893, when records were first kept there, it has been struck by tornadoes an unbelievable 193 times.

What IS It about Florida and Hurricanes?

Over the last century, more than 60 hurricanes have struck the state of Florida, making it the undisputed, world champion, hurricane hotspot. The storms can come in from three directions — south, east and west — usually during hurricane season, from June to November. On average, Florida gets hit once every two years.

But that's on average. At the extreme end of the records, you can find the year 2004, when three full-fledged hurricanes hit the state within 21 days. It was an unprecedented string that left residents with billions of dollars of damage and scientists with a difficult but deeply important meteorological question, which can best be paraphrased as, "What's going on?"

Orlando

Tampa

Miami

How to Cook a Hurricane

If you think of the tropical seas as steaming pots of water cooked by the sun and stirred by the turning of the Earth itself, you'll understand the basic recipe for hurricanes. Hurricanes are born and sustained by warm water and they die within a few days of leaving it.

Most Atlantic Ocean hurricanes start as storm "seedlings" that form in late summer off the coast of West Africa. These storms travel west, often growing in strength as they feed on the warm ocean water.

The winds start to spiral as a result of the earth's rotation. The storm grows and grows, finally hitting wind speeds of 74 mph (119 km/h) or more. It is now officially a hurricane.

Cross Section of a Hurricane

Cooled air plunges down to be warmed.

At the center is an eye of calm.

Bands of rain and intense wind spiral around the eye.

Air warmed by the ocean spirals upward.

Hurricane birds, the Lockheed P-3 Orion

Why You Don't Want to Fly in These Planes

In 1943, an Air Force pilot by the name of Joseph Duckworth decided (all on his own) to do what no one had ever done before: fly an airplane straight through the outer wall of a hurricane and right into its eye. His single-engine trainer was thrown around the sky like a toy, but Duckworth managed to get into the calm of the storm's center where he reported blue sky above and an incredibly tortured sea below.

Duckworth got a medal for his flight, and a small band of derring-do pilots were recruited by the National Weather Service to invent the fine art of hurricane flying while gathering meteorological data.

One veteran hurricaner, Commander David Turner, was once interviewed about a particularly rough mission into Hurricane Edith: "It was a bit more than the ordinary flight. In fact, we got the living daylights beaten out of us. We were jerked around so violently that I couldn't tell which way was up — all the dials were going nuts." Shortly after landing, Turner re-fueled and went right back up ("We just wanted to verify it had been that rough"). He was once asked why he volunteered for the flights (the money isn't that good); "Oh, it's interesting work," he replied.

Another military pilot, Bill Rankin, showed how you could fly even without the benefit of an airplane (something that people used to think was impossible).

Rankin's jet lost an engine over Virginia in 1959 and he had to eject right over the heart of a violent thunderstorm. The moment his parachute opened, he found (to his surprise) that he was going up (not down) at a terrific rate. Here is how he described the experience:

"I went soaring up and up... buffeted in all directions — up, down, sideways, clockwise, counterclockwise, over and over. I was stretched, slammed and pounded like a bag of flesh crashing into concrete. Meanwhile, it was raining so hard, I thought I would drown in mid-air."

Bill Rankin's airplane-less stormy flight appears to be unique. At least, no one else has ever come back down to Earth in a condition to talk about any similar experience.

BEFORE >

The Story of Hurricane Camille and

When civil defense authorities issue a hurricane evacuation order, there are always a few thrill-seekers who deliberately ignore the warnings. Instead, they plant themselves right in the hurricane's path and hope to get a really close look at really big weather.

Molly Blackenstone (not her real name) was one of those people. In 1969 she

and a group of about 20 friends decided to disregard evacuation warnings and gather for a "hurricane party" on the third floor of their apartment building. Not a good idea.

Hurricane Camille was a Class V hurricane, with core winds of 200 mph (about 320 km/h). In a sudden change of direction, the storm took dead-aim at their little town of Pass Christian, Mississippi.

AFTER >

the Former Richelieu Apartment Building

Molly never even got to the party. She and her husband were still in their apartment when the picture window blew out ("We heard an awful popping sound"). Moments later, both of them had their shoulders pressed against the door, trying to keep out the wind and water.

It was hopeless. The entire building began to rock ("It felt like we were in a boat"). Molly's last glimpse of her apartment building came as she swam through her second-story window, washed out on the storm surge.

Exactly what happened next is not entirely clear. Molly was found in a tree more than 5 miles (8 km) from the former Richelieu apartment building, miraculously alive. In an interview afterward, she stated that during the next hurricane watch, "I'm leaving along with the rest of them."

Katrina: The Hurricane That Changed Everything

On August 23, 2005, the National Hurricane Center in Miami, Florida, began tracking an ordinary tropical depression located in the mid-Atlantic Ocean. On August 25, it reached the East Coast of Florida as a low Category 1 storm, causing moderate damage. On August 26 it crossed into the Gulf of Mexico and there, over the warm Gulf waters, began a staggering transformation. By August 28, in only 48 hours, it had changed dramatically, growing into a certified monster, a Category 5 super-storm, the highest ranking possible. Winds were in excess of 175 mph, making it one of the most intense storms ever bred in the Atlantic Ocean and one that was destined to be the most significant storm in modern American history.

Hurricane Katrina reached the Louisiana coast on August 29. Winds were in excess of 120 mph but the real damage came as a consequence of a 15-foot "storm surge," a kind of super-tide driven by the intense winds.

The city of New Orleans is one of the original cities in the United States, dating from the early 18th century. It is a port located on the low Mississippi River delta and as a result it has been subject to periodic flooding throughout its history. Understandably, the oldest parts of the city were constructed on the highest ground. But as the city grew, extensive construction took place in areas that were actually below sea level and protected from flooding by walls of earth, the famous levees of New Orleans.

Hurricane Katrina in its Class 5 phase in the Gulf of Mexico.

Building like this sounds a bit riskier and more uncommon than it actually is. In Europe and Asia, millions of people live in levee-protected areas that are below sea level. The city of Venice is probably the most famous example of all, but significant parts of Belgium and Holland share this same reality as well.

The system of levees that protected New Orleans was designed to withstand a surge that might accompany a direct hit from a Category 3 storm, not unlike Katrina. However, for many years, public safety experts have questioned that estimate and have often described a major New Orleans hurricane right there along with a San Francisco earthquake as the two most frightening — and likely — North American disasters.

In any event, all the guessing was put aside on August 29 when the surge from Katrina hit and the levee system failed in more than 40 places, putting the city of New Orleans essentially underwater (80% flooded, to be precise). More than 1,800 people lost their lives and damage has been estimated at $81.2 billion dollars, making it the costliest natural disaster in U.S. history.

In the process, New Orleans became the first major U.S. city to be ordered evacuated in 200 years.

The effects of this unprecedented disaster will be felt for decades to come. The city of New Orleans will be rebuilt over time, and no doubt regain much if not all of its pre-storm population. But there will be many permanent changes as well. The levee system will have to be substantially upgraded (a multi-billion dollar federal public works project that will not be funded without much controversy). Parts of the city may be described as "permanent floodplain" and may never see new construction. The delta eco-system has been severely changed, not just by the storm, but by the levee system

The path of Hurricane Katrina. August 25 – August 31, 2005.

as well. Economically, the area may never regain its pre-storm status. Since the city of New Orleans was and is largely populated by African-Americans, the elements of race and poverty have been mixed into the after-storm debate about responsibility and prevention. Politically, that factor will have a near- and long-term effect on elections, and not just locally.

Today, the word "Katrina" no longer refers just to a hurricane that struck the Louisiana coast in the summer of 2005, but to a change in America and a perceived change in nature. It has become a watershed event. We are now, all of us, post-Katrina, and hopefully, that means we will now, all of us, be better citizens of the planet and better citizens of the country.

The Hurricane Hall of Fame and Facts

The University of Miami mascot is the ibis, which is the last bird to leave before a hurricane arrives and the first bird to come back when it leaves.

Strongest Hurricane of All Time?

Hurricane Gilbert had recorded winds of 218 mph (350 km/h) when it struck Northern Mexico in 1988. The pressure inside Gilbert was the lowest ever recorded by meteorologists.

Deadliest Hurricane in North American History?

Probably the hurricane that hit Galveston, Texas, on September 8, 1900. As the winds built up early in the day, people streamed to the beach to see the huge waves. A surge of water pushed ahead of the hurricane and soon children were playing in flooded yards. But the fun stopped with the arrival of the full force of the hurricane and the flooding. In 24 hours, the entire city was underwater, leaving 15 percent of the population dead.

Galveston was rebuilt. A huge sea wall was constructed. And 2000 buildings were jacked up above sea level, with the land filled in under them, so that such destruction could never happen again.

Jupiter's Great Red Spot is approximately three Earths wide.

Shown to scale

Biggest Hurricane of All?

On the planet Jupiter, they know how to make hurricanes. Or at least things that look like hurricanes. The Jovian whirlwind shown here, called the Great Red Spot, was first seen by Galileo 300 years ago. It's still spinning today.

The Name Game

For a long time, all hurricanes were given girls' names. That changed in 1979 with the first "boy" hurricane — Bob. Today, official policy is to alternate.

A really big hurricane may have its name "retired" (never used again) — as when a sports hero retires and takes his jersey number with him.

P.S. Hurricanes are called typhoons in other parts of the world. Both hurricanes and typhoons are tropical cyclones.

Q: Are there hurricanes at the equator?

A: The experts said no —

the equator has the warm waters that can give birth to hurricanes, but not the spinning winds. Then, on December 27, 2001, the experts were proved wrong. Typhoon Vamei developed over the equator in the South China Sea near Singapore.

Now You Know Why They Call Them Mobile Homes.

Mobile homes have a mysterious sort of reputation for attracting tornadoes and hurricanes since the after-storm news shows are often filled with pictures of flipped and smashed RVs. But the real story has less to do with the Twilight Zone and more to do with building codes. Mobile homes don't have foundations and make very poor storm shelters.

What Happens When a Hurricane Hits a Children's Book Publishing Company?

Florida has had its fill of doom-and-gloom weather forecasters with predictions of disaster that never materialized. But on August 13, 2004, all that changed as Hurricane Charley stunned South and Central Florida with a wicked left uppercut that knocked down thousands of trees and left millions of residents without power. Many of us at Scholastic in Lake Mary, Florida, were caught flat-footed. Despite dire warnings, we just knew this was going to be one more in a long series of false alarms. Sure, we'd get some wind and rain, but we'd had daily thunderstorms do more damage than recent hurricanes. But Charley was a wake-up call. Many of us couldn't even leave our homes. And it came at one of our busiest times of the year: In just a few days, dozens of book experts and publishing companies were gathering in Orlando to select the books that would appear in the upcoming Scholastic Book Fairs.

We had hardly had a chance to regroup with new appointments and travel plans when Hurricane Frances threw a very slow right hook at us on September 5, causing extensive flooding. And finally, wandering Hurricane Jeanne hit us with a strong right cross three weeks later, disrupting school schedules and wreaking havoc with our Book Fair events. Charley, Frances and Jeanne were the second, fourth and eighth costliest hurricanes in U.S. history. **OUCH!**

(For the answer to the related question, "What would happen to a children's book publishing company if it were hit by an earthquake?" turn to page 35.)

Earthquakes Come In  Styles

The plates of the Earth's crust are straining against one another in constant gridlock. When the strain breaks, the movement is sharp and sudden. The damage to the crust is seen along faults.

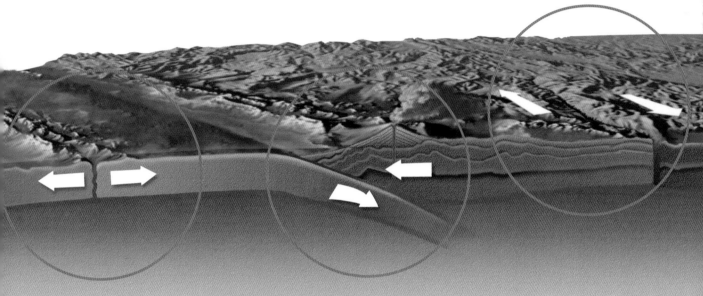

PULLING APART

Plates can pull apart or get pushed apart by hot liquid material surging up from under the Earth's crust. Africa's Great Rift Valley is one place this has happened. Millions of years from now, the movement of the plates may rip the continent of Africa in two along this rift.

HEAD-ON COLLISION

When plates collide, the edges sometimes crumple up into mountain ranges. Or one plate can dive under the other. Sounds smooth but it isn't. Plates can get stuck and energy builds until it is finally released in an earthquake.

SIDESWIPE

A sideswipe means two plates are trying to slide by each other. They stick and grind and it's energy build-up time again. California's San Andreas fault is one example of sideswiping plates. Major earthquakes have rumbled California along this fault.

How to Predict An Earthquake

Early on the morning of February 4, 1975, Chinese officials ordered the inhabitants of Liaoning province into the streets. An earthquake, they warned, was about to happen. All day the townspeople waited in the bitter cold. Then just after 7:30 pm, it struck. Hundreds of empty houses collapsed in a major quake.

Losing homes was bad news, but predicting when a quake would happen was great news.

Unfortunately, it turned out to be an unrepeatable fluke. Since then, using the same techniques, the Chinese have predicted dozens of quakes that haven't happened and failed to predict a few that did.

Today, most scientists don't think it is possible to predict the exact day or even month an earthquake may happen.

But some are not willing to give up without a fight. The Chinese are the world's leaders in earthquake prediction optimism. Chinese scientists continue to make specific earthquake forecasts. Everyone else in the world settles for statistical likelihoods over long periods of time.

Does Odd Animal Behavior Predict Earthquakes?

People have long believed that weird animal behavior may signal an upcoming earthquake. This is not junk science. There have been many well-documented reports of odd animal behavior before a quake.

Unfortunately, as pet owners everywhere will be happy to tell you, animals behave in weird ways all the time, earthquakes or not. Nevertheless, the Chinese are convinced there's a link. They maintain an animal earthquake prediction facility with 24-hour video cameras on their subjects, just waiting for the first signs of pre-quake critter jitters.

Millions of booklets with pictures like these are distributed in China telling the populace to be on the look-out for jumping catfish, rearing horses and stampeding pigs. The theory? Animals can sense earthquakes coming.

What Happens When an Earthquake Hits a Children's Book Publishing Company?

This used to be an area of research filled with little but speculation since scientists had precious little data to work with. But at 5:04 pm on October 17, 1989, centuries of guesswork came to a sudden conclusion when Klutz Galactic Headquarters in Palo Alto, California was rocked by the Loma Prieta earthquake (epicenter, 31 miles south). Here, finally, are the answers to this ancient question, provided by first-hand witnesses (us).

When the walls began to shake, everybody inside the building broke into three camps: One group ran outside, another group got under their desks and a third group (the largest) couldn't decide and so began to debate the issue.

Meanwhile, since one of us happened to be on the phone to a customer about 40 miles north, we were able to give them helpful advance notice by suddenly yelling into the phone the approved earthquake alert: "Eeeeeeeek! Eeeeek! An earthquake!"

In this way, we proved that earthquakes do travel slower than phone calls — but not by much. In a follow-up call a few days later, we learned that our customer's walls began shaking about 4 seconds after he got our warning. (Knowing that an earthquake travels 40 miles in 4 seconds is useful information for people who've ever thought about outrunning a quake.)

After the shaking stopped (15 seconds?) and the various groups managed to find themselves, we discovered that the damage was gratefully minimal — some fallen books, a knocked-over cardboard display, one deeply traumatized office cat. Meanwhile, houses and buildings located less than a mile away suffered serious structural damage. (It turns out that our building is located on bedrock, not shake-able unstable soil.) Nevertheless, we spent the next 6 months installing additional steel inside the building, losing a good bit of window glass but gaining a needed measure of security in the process.

(For the answer to the related question, "What would happen to a children's book publishing company if it were hit by a hurricane?", turn to page 29.)

100% KLUTZ CERTIFIED

A Before & After Earthquake Photo Album

◀ **BEFORE**   **AFTER** ▶

In this picture, a statue on the Stanford University campus was knocked down by the 1906 San Francisco earthquake. (P.S. The statue was of Louis Agassiz, a vocal opponent of evolution. As someone remarked at the time, "Agassiz was better in the abstract than in the concrete.")

P.S. We cheated and added the graduate to these pictures. But the story is true.

◀ **BEFORE**   **AFTER** ▶

In earthquake country, putting buildings on stilts to allow for ground level parking is bad design. The stilts tend to buckle when the quake hits. Building codes in Los Angeles (home to this building) and throughout California have been toughened since the 1994 Northridge quake, making this kind of construction illegal.

◀ **BEFORE**   **AFTER** ▶

Assuming they aren't on an overpass (or under a building like this one was), cars are pretty good earthquake shelters. Thousands of motorists simultaneously pulled over during the California Loma Prieta quake in 1989 and checked their tires, mistaking the earthquake for nothing more than a flat.

EARTHQUAKE *Trivia*

Fire!

Fires fed by broken gas mains roared out of control in San Francisco the night after the quake of 1989. The section of the city shown here is built on unstable debris and landfill (some of which was created by the 1906 earthquake). The soil liquefied in a way that solid bedrock cannot, and the damage here was the most extensive of anywhere in the city.

Roaches to the Rescue

Trained rescue dogs are often too big to crawl through the worst parts of collapsed buildings in search of survivors. So, Japanese scientists have outfitted roaches with backpacks containing battery-powered radios and mini-microphones. Their hope? Launch squadrons of Rescue Roaches into the buildings and monitor their radios for sounds of survivors. We are not making this up.

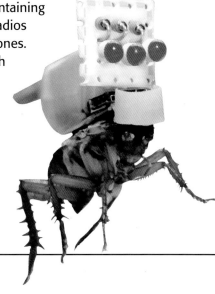

Let Sleeping Elephants Lie

Long before modern science figured out what was really going on, there were many, many theories about what caused earthquakes (nobody who lives in earthquake country ignores them). In India, at one time, people believed that eight strong elephants held up the Earth. If one got sleepy and laid down for a nap, the Earth shook.

Do-It-Yourself Earthquake

What would happen if billions of disciplined Chinese got into a crouch and, at a nation-wide broadcasted signal, leapt into the air all at once? Would the impact of their landing be enough to send a shock wave through the Earth's crust and trigger North American earthquake faults? This intriguing question was investigated in 1969 by a couple of Earth scientists whose results were reported in TIME Magazine. The answer is no. You may sleep easy again.

December 26, 2004

Tsunami Strikes Asia & Africa

INDIAN OCEAN

Dec. 26, 2004 — On December 26, 2004, the worst tsunami ever recorded hit coastal towns all over southeast Asia and parts of Africa, flattening homes and sweeping people and belongings out to sea.

An earthquake in the Indian Ocean (at the red dot on this map) started the tsunami. The earthquake thrust up the seafloor, forcing the water above it up too. The bulge of water fanned out in a series of huge waves which destroyed everything in their path.

Hour after hour, the tsunami waves rippled outward, slamming into islands and other land forms.

Finally, seven hours after it started, the tsunami hit the coast of Africa. In all, more than 200,000 people were killed in more than 10 countries.

Deadliest Natural Disaster in Almost 30 Years

Earthquake-triggered tsunami waves hitting Kammale temple in Phuket, Thailand.

First Person
One Survivor's Story

PHUKET, THAILAND
Dec. 26, 2004 — Troy Husum had left the cold Canadian winter behind to vacation in Phuket [poo-ket], Thailand. It seemed like paradise, until 9:15 on the morning of December 26.

Troy was standing on his hotel balcony, when he felt a mild earthquake. No one seemed worried, so Troy ignored it. Then things started to get weird.

"About 45 minutes later, I noticed the water had receded from Patong Bay. We'd never seen it before, and we could hear people on the beach talking about it. You could even see fish flopping around on the beach, which was unusual.

"Then I saw it — I noticed people craning their necks and looking out to the horizon. You could see a wall of water about three or four stories high."

The wall of water swept over the beach and just kept coming. It bent trees, picked up beach umbrellas and cars — anything in its path. Troy ran up to the roof of his hotel, but the water kept rising. ("It flowed up to the third floor, you could see it in the stairwell.") When it was over, Troy ventured outside. "It looked like a bomb had gone off."

A City Uncovered
SOUTHEAST INDIA

On the southeast coast of India lies the remains of the ancient city of Mahabalipuram. The city, a collection of temples, is a popular tourist attraction. But it turns out that there was more to the city hidden under the sea.

When the tsunami of December 26, 2004, battered the area, it did archaeologists a favor and uncovered two carved structures that had been buried in sand and water. Ancient stone lions and horses saw the light of day for the first time in many centuries, all thanks to the tsunami.

How Tsunamis Start

A tsunami starts with a huge shake-up of the sea floor. An undersea earthquake, volcano or landslide thrusts up the water above it and sends enormous waves spreading outward. The tsunami waves can travel for thousands of miles, but it is usually only when they hit land that they become deadly.

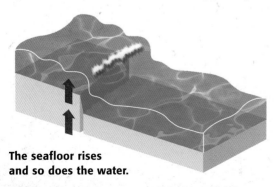

The seafloor rises and so does the water.

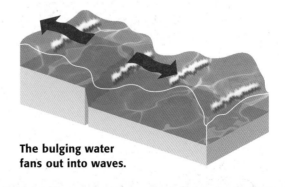

The bulging water fans out into waves.

The Power of the Ocean

No, he didn't see it coming. Yes, he did escape back through the doorway and closed the door in time. Whew!

TSUNAMI *Trivia*

ANCIENT TRIBAL FOLKLORE STORIES SAVE LIVES

On the small Andaman Islands just north of the earthquake epicenter there are ancient tribes whose folklore stories talk of "huge shaking of ground followed by high wall of water." This was an early warning system for them; these stories that passed from generation to generation taught people how to act in an emergency.

They went quickly to higher ground after the earthquake and saved themselves from the tsunami. Old stories saved them!

HOW OFTEN?

Ten or so tsunamis hit somewhere on Earth every year. Most do no damage.

WHAT'S IT LIKE FOR THE BOATS AT SEA?

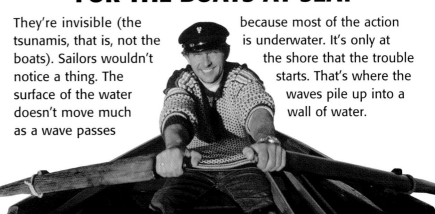

They're invisible (the tsunamis, that is, not the boats). Sailors wouldn't notice a thing. The surface of the water doesn't move much as a wave passes because most of the action is underwater. It's only at the shore that the trouble starts. That's where the waves pile up into a wall of water.

HOW FAST?

A tsunami travels at approximately 600 mph (966 km/h) across deep ocean. About the same speed as a jetliner.

On August 26, 1883, the Indonesian island of **KRAKATAU** was the site of the second largest volcanic eruption in recorded history. The explosion and subsequent collapse of the volcano triggered a tsunami that wiped out 165 coastal towns.

Compared to a tsunami, this is just
A Tiny Wave

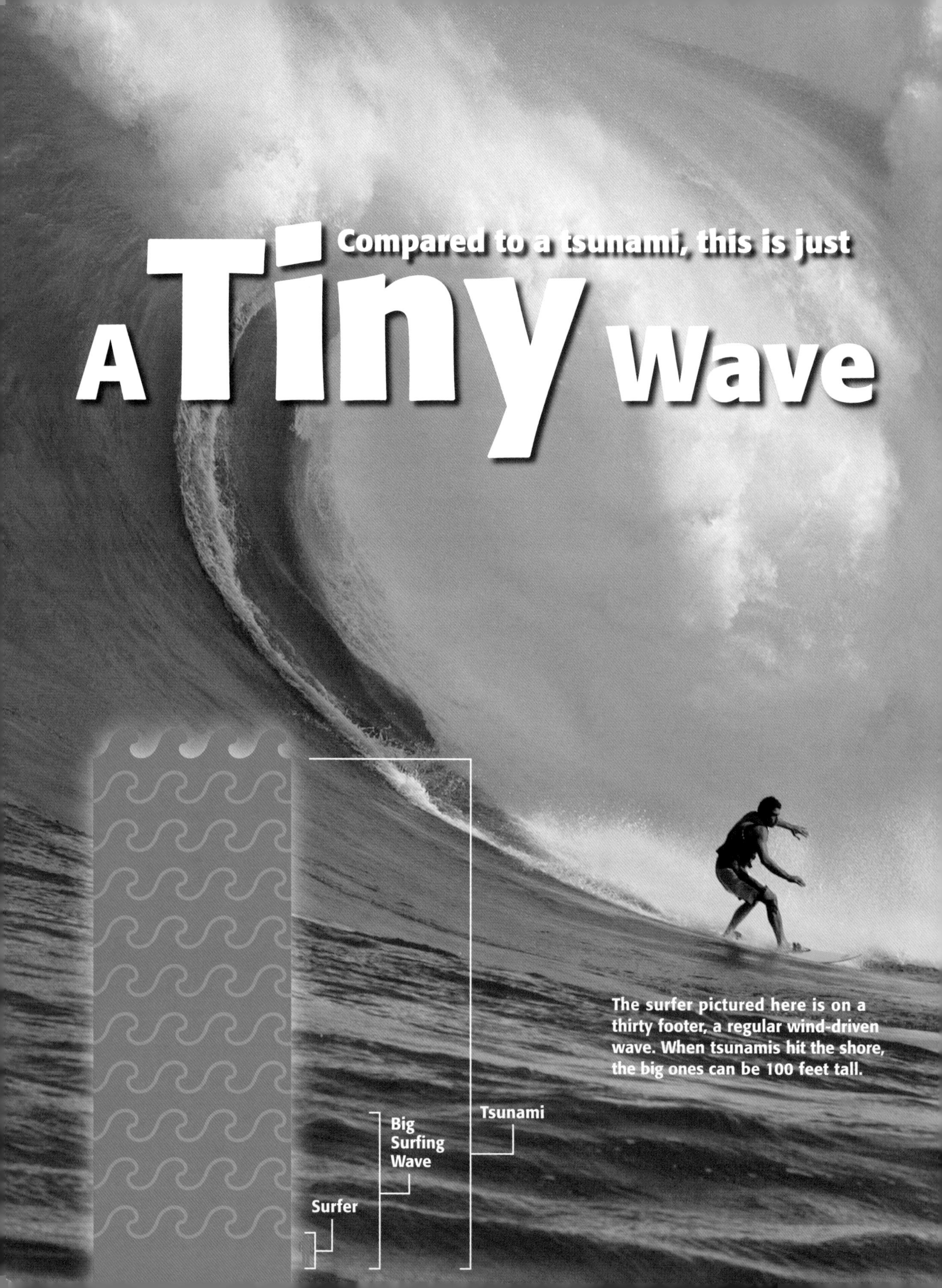

The surfer pictured here is on a thirty footer, a regular wind-driven wave. When tsunamis hit the shore, the big ones can be 100 feet tall.

Tsunami

Big
Surfing
Wave

Surfer

Is It Possible to Surf a Tsunami?

Out of the many unbelievable stories that came from the December 2004 Indian Ocean tsunami, was this one:

Surfer Martin Hambrook, 40, from Porthcawl, South Wales, was in the sea off the island's southern coast waiting for what he hoped would be a perfect wave.

Partner Vicky Maxwell, 42, and son Jai, 7, were watching from the beach as the horrific form of the tsunami appeared on the horizon.

"As an experienced surfer, when I saw the wave come, I realized something was wrong, but I couldn't escape because the surfboard was tied to my ankle." Despite the ferocity of the wave, Hambrook stayed on his board as he was carried over the sandy beach right up to the hotel.

He leapt off by a restaurant as the sea withdrew and a second wave, about 30 feet (10 meters) high, rolled in. The family then fled to higher ground where all three survived.

Rogue Waves

The photo here shows three men nailing plywood over windows. They had their backs to the surf, something that lifeguards will tell you is not recommended. The wave that crashed into them was far bigger than anything else around it.

Volcanoes

The volcano shown here doesn't exist anymore. It vanished — or at least a fair chunk of it vanished — during a spectacular eruption one horrendous day about 7,000 years ago.

In the months after the eruption, Mt. Mazama's dome collapsed, leaving a bowl-shaped crater. Rainwater gradually filled the crater to a depth of 4,000 feet (1200 m), creating a lake. Today Crater Lake, as it is now called, is one of the most popular National Parks. You can visit it in Oregon.

Our planet is Volcano Central. As you read this, 20 or so volcanoes are erupting somewhere on the Earth. The planet is studded with about 500 active volcanoes, and 50 or more erupt each year. Some volcanoes are one-day wonders. Others, like Stromboli volcano in Italy, have been erupting for thousands of years.

Volcanoes are holes or tears in the Earth's crust out of which hot lava, gases and ash ooze or shoot. When that happens, stand back. Way back.

A Volcano
X-Ray

It's tall, it's steep-sided and it's ready to blow. It's a stratovolcano, the most common kind of volcano on the Earth and one of the most explosive. A stratovolcano can shoot ash, cinders and lava skyward. And it can send a deadly mix of gases, ash and rock, called a pyroclastic flow, racing down its slopes at hurricane speeds. When a stratovolcano erupts, it's best to be somewhere (anywhere) else.

2 If a vent gets plugged with magma, the pressure builds until finally — kablam! The magma is blasted into ash and cinders and shoots out of the volcano.

3 Ash, cinders and molten lava build up over time, forming a cone.

1 Molten magma from under the Earth's rocky crust oozes up through one or more vents.

The Volcano Hall of Fame and Facts

The Mexican Insta-Volcano

In February 1943, a patch of Mexican cornfield suddenly started belching out smoke, then lava. By the next day, a mini-volcano had formed. And Paricutin (or El Monstruo, as the locals call it) just kept growing. Today, the volcano-that-started-as-a-cornfield is 1345 feet (410 m) tall.

Nobody Got Hurt

This abandoned school bus was swallowed by lava flowing from a Hawaiian volcano. Some lava flows easily, while other lava is thick and gooey. The temperature of lava varies, depending on its chemical composition, but it can reach 2000°F (1100°C).

Volcanic Bombs

Erupting volcanoes can launch rocks and blobs of molten rock into the air as "volcanic bombs." The crust of a lava bomb cools as it flies through the air and the bomb often turns teardrop-shaped. Scientists who study volcanoes up close like to wear helmets and fireproof "anti–volcanic-bomb" shoulder pads.

Airplanes and Volcanoes

In 1982, an eruption in Galunggung, West Java, threw volcanic ash more than 25,000 feet (7600 m) into the air. The engines on two jetliners flying over the eruption conked out in the cloud of ash, and both planes fell thousands of feet before the pilots were able to re-start them, narrowly avoiding a tragedy. Because of such dangers, airspace over active volcanoes is off-limits to commercial aircraft.

Black Smokers

Just about the weirdest life ever discovered on planet Earth is located on the bottom of the oceans. It's found at cracks on the seafloor that expose the molten magma under the Earth's crust and spew out ash and super-heated water. A very strange ecosystem has evolved beside these cracks, made up of horror-movie kinds of things that no one has seen at the surface. They get their energy not from the sun but from the hot chemical-filled water that rises from the cracks. Should the sun ever blink out, the life forms with the best chance of survival will be life that has evolved down here.

The Story of Pompeii

These are not the bodies of Pompeii's victims, but modern plaster casts. They were created by archaeologists who poured plaster into cavities left by the actual bodies.

In the year 79 AD, Pompeii was a village near Mount Vesuvius, on the coast on Italy. When Mt. Vesuvius erupted on August 25th of that year, the town and 3,360 people in it were wiped out.

Many inhabitants were suffocated by poisonous fumes as they fled their homes, and then covered with a layer of ash and mud.

Over the years, their bodies decayed, leaving only bones and body-shaped holes in the hardened mud. In 1860, an Italian scientist discovered a way to fill the holes with plaster. Hundreds of plaster casts have since been taken of the Pompeii citizens, some of them showing enough detail to be recognizable individuals.

Mt. Vesuvius has erupted several times since it blotted out Pompeii, and nearby Mt. Aetna is also still active.

ITALY

Pompeii

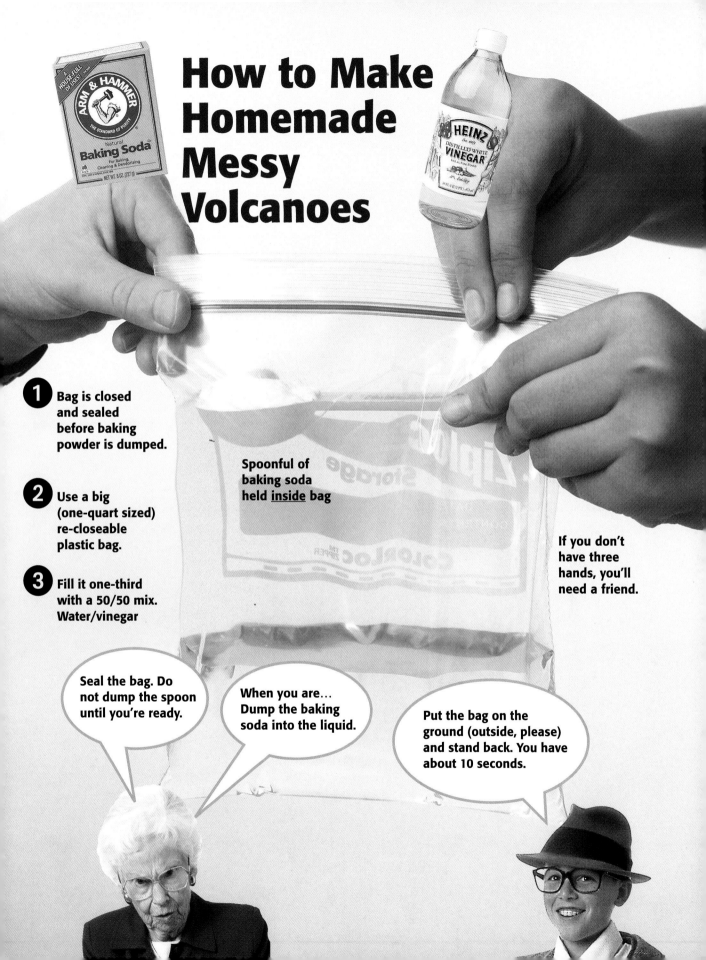

The Story of Mount St. Helens

In March 1980, Mt. St. Helens in Washington State began sending out a message that it was no longer a sleeping giant. Earthquakes shook the volcano, which had been dormant for more than a century. Puffs of smoke emerged and its peak sunk, forming a huge crater. Most ominous was a bulge high on the mountain's north side. It grew by about 5 feet (1.5 m) a day.

At first, local residents were nervous, especially when they were ordered to evacuate. But as the mountain continued to rumble and grumble for an amazing two months, people demanded to get back into their homes. Except for a few daredevil news helicopters, the journalists also packed it in. And many of the scientists were sent home.

Then on May 18, a huge earthquake rumbled under the mountain and the bulge tore away, creating the largest landslide ever recorded. A fiery hot blast of gases, steam and rocks flattened or burned everything in its path. The heat melted snow and ice, sending torrents of water and mud down the mountain at breakneck speeds. A plume of ash shot 12 miles (19 km) into the atmosphere.

When it was all over, Mt. St. Helens was missing the top 1312 feet (400 m), and a good part of the rest of the mountain looked like it belonged on the moon. Ash from the eruption fell over much of the western U.S. and Canada. And the giant has not gone back to sleep. Rumbling and belching smoke from time to time, Mt. St. Helens continues to keep its neighbors on their toes.

BEFORE >

AFTER >

Donna and Steve at White Island Volcano in New Zealand.

A Volcanic Relationship

When Donna and Steve O'Meara got married, the bride wore sneakers and the happy pair arrived at the celebration in a helicopter. Partway through the ceremony, the bride's sneakers started to melt. No wonder: The O'Mearas were married on an active volcano.

"It was my wedding. And my sneakers were melting."

The O'Mearas are hooked on volcanoes. Donna is a volcanologist, a scientist who studies volcanoes. Steve is an astronomer who studies how planets form, including their volcanoes. When they hear a volcano is erupting somewhere on the Earth, they grab their gear and go.

That's when things start getting interesting. They hike up volcanoes and hang out on the rim, studying and shooting the eruption. Lava bombs, scalding steam and hissing magma are all in a day's work for Steve and Donna. They're so nuts about volcanoes, they even live by one, in the town of Volcano, Hawaii, just at the edge of Kilauea volcano.

Floods

Most people describe a flood as simply more water than they want, in places where they don't need it. It's actually a good working definition since floods are hardly freaks of nature. On a planet that's already two-thirds covered with water, the fact that the other third gets washed over from time to time shouldn't come as any huge surprise.

Floods kill more people every year in North America than any other kind of natural disaster. Most floods come on fairly slowly as rivers crest above their banks. These kinds of "slow" floods are civil enough to allow time for residents to evacuate. But when the water recedes, it leaves behind a lot of mud and a mess that can take months to clean up.

In 1993, months of unrelenting rain led to a phenomenal once-in-500-years flood that overwhelmed 50 years' worth of levee construction in eight states throughout most of the Lower Mississippi River region. It was the most damaging natural disaster in modern North American history. Among the losers were the Quad City River Bandits in Davenport, Iowa, whose baseball stadium is pictured here.

Early settlers in what is now Winnipeg, Manitoba, Canada, were warned by natives that the Red River was unpredictable and dangerous. Many regretted ignoring those warnings when the 10-year settlement became submerged in over 36 feet (11 m) of water in 1826. Other major floods followed in 1948, 1950 and 1997.

At the end of the Great Ice Age about 20,000 years ago a giant lake formed near what is now Spokane, Washington. Half the size of Lake Michigan, it was contained by an ice dam that eventually broke under pressure. The water drained into the Spokane Valley at a rate of speed about 10 times the combined flow of all the world's rivers!

Residents of the small steel town of Johnstown, Pennsylvania, had always been aware of flood risks: The town was built on a flood plain. However, nothing could prepare them for the May afternoon in 1889 when the wooden dam just upriver broke and unleashed the waters of Lake Conemaugh. The rushing water wiped out the town, killing over 2,000 people and leaving many more homeless.

Q:
What Happens When You Mix Water and Dirt?

A:
You get MUD and grown men in suits, like Harrold Weinstein here, want to play in it, at least they do in the annual North Conway, New Hampshire, Mud Bowl.

In 1927 the Mississippi River overflowed its banks and flooded 27,000 square miles in 30 feet of water. The Great Mississippi Flood, as it is known, was the most destructive in U.S. history.

Flash Floods

Flash floods are hit-and-run rogues. They can turn a dry gully into a raging torrent in little more than a minute. They usually occur when a thunderstorm stalls out and drenches one small area. That's what happened in Kinlochrannoch, Scotland, where this picture was taken.

These photographs of a house caving in were taken during a flash flood in Tucson, Arizona, in October 1982. Flash floods are particularly common in desert country because of the nature of desert soil — hard-packed and free of plant life. The rain will hit and run if the soil is unable to soak it up.

The Hall of Flood Fame and Facts

The Forecast Called for Scattered Showers

It turned out to be a lot more than that. A flood that experts described as a once-in-a-century event nearly washed Rapid City, South Dakota, right off the map in June 1972. One woman found her car in a tree. Another discovered her house had floated to a brand new address. More than 200 people died. Today, in Rapid City, residents talk about the years B.F. (Before the Flood) and A.F. (After the Flood).

The Boston Molasses Flood

On January 15, 1919, an enormous tank full of molasses exploded at the Purity Distilling Company in Boston, Massachusetts.

A two-story wave of molasses roared into a residential area, killing 21 people and three horses. There are residents of Boston alive today who still cannot stand the smell of molasses.

The Missoula High Football Team (Class of 13,000 B.C.)

Missoula, Montana, used to be underneath a deep lake held in place by a monstrous dam of ice. In one phenomenal meltdown (15,000 years ago), the dam gave way and a flood of incredible size inundated most of what is now eastern Washington State. The geologist J. Harlen Bretz, who first proposed this catastrophic flood theory, was widely ridiculed for it (geologists tend to think in terms of millennia, not Big Days). He was finally vindicated, years later, when giant ripple marks up to 30 feet (9m) high were found.

Putnam, Connecticut, 1955

This incredible photograph was taken August 19, 1955, in Putnam, Connecticut. Two rivers run through Putnam and in 1955 they were held in check by a series of earthen dams. Hurricane Diane and a torrential downpour proved too much for the old dams and they broke like a row of falling dominoes. The resulting wave of water came down Main Street like a runaway train. A factory in town manufactured magnesium, a chemical that burns underwater. When the factory walls collapsed, barrels of magnesium were swept away, exploding like bombs as they went.

Historic Floods

Guidry's Cajun restaurant is closed due to high ▶ water from the River Des Peres in south St. Louis on July 18, 1993. Most of this south St. Louis neighborhood was destroyed during the Great Flood of 1993.

◀ High Tide

These kids are testing out their wet weather gear in the Piazza San Marco in Venice, Italy. Normally, the piazza is a stone-dry square. But Venice is an island city at the edge of the Adriatic Sea, and when the tides rise, watch out. The Italians call it acqua alta, which means high water. In 1966 the acqua got so alta that more than 3 feet (1 m) of salty seawater sloshed over parts of the city, turning the Piazza San Marco into a giant wading pool.

"A Roar Like Thunder" ▶

Thunder is what it sounded like when the South Fork Dam broke and sent a wall of water smashing into the sleepy town of Johnstown, Pennsylvania, on May 31, 1889. Rocks, trees and chunks of buildings churned in the water, which raced downhill at 40 mph (65 km/h). In just 10 minutes, the downtown was destroyed, and many people were swept to their deaths. Then debris that piled up against an old bridge caught on fire, killing many more. When it was all over, the flood had the highest death toll in U.S. history. More than 2200 were dead or missing.

◀ Fire and Flood

In April 1997, Grand Forks, North Dakota, had a once-in-500-year flood. From the air, houses looked like houseboats bobbing at sea. But the flood wasn't the only problem. Floodwaters knocked down power lines, which short circuited, starting fires in the downtown area.

You'd think all that water would make it easy to put out a fire. But there was just too much water. Firefighters had to slosh through chest-deep water just to get to the fires. When it was all over, nine historic buildings had burned down in a sea of water.

Ever Wonder What Would Happen If You Left the Sink Running for a Weekend?

A regular faucet can put out about 200 gallons (750 L) per hour. Leave it turned on for a weekend and, if your house is watertight and about average size, come Sunday night, you could be unlocking the door to 5 feet (1.5 m) of water.

This picture is a fake. Much as we would have liked to have really done it when we were kids, none of our mothers would let us try

it and besides, nobody's house is watertight or strong enough to work like a barrel and really contain that much water. Disappointing, but it brings up an interesting point.

Water is heavy stuff. Ask anybody who's ever had to carry a bucket of it. Try to turn your living room into a swimming pool and you'll blow the walls out.